# I Am Ok

POEMS OF GRACE

## Gwendolyn M Lacy

Gwendolyn M Lacy/Rejoice Essential Publishing
PO BOX 512
Effingham, SC 29541
www.republishing.org

Unless otherwise indicated, scripture is taken from the King James Version.

**I Am Ok/Gwendolyn M Lacy**

ISBN-13: 978-1-956775-69-3

"I am a believer not because of anything I read or heard but solely on my personal experiences."

Gwendolyn Lacy

# Dedication

I WOULD LIKE TO dedicate this book to my father, John Robert Lacy, my mother Annie Thomas, and my children, JerAnthony and Kandee. I love you all dearly.

# Table of Contents

# Acknowledgments

IRST AND FOREMOST, I give thanks to the Almighty God for my gift of writing. I want to give acknowledgment to my dear friend and sister in Christ, Tiffany McClure. We met through You-Tube and instantly were divinely connected. Thank you, Tiffany, for allowing the Lord to speak life into me by you believing in my gift, a friend is a true blessing and I'm grateful for our friendship.

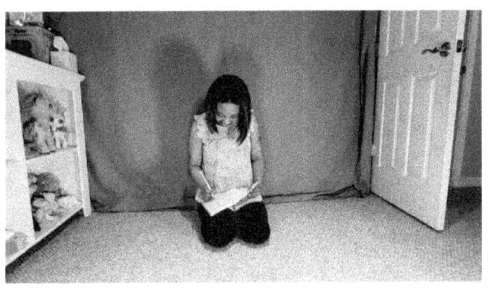

I Am Ok

POEM 1

# GOD'S LOVE

LESSINGS FROM HIGH ABOVE
Vibe with me for a moment. Let's
talk about love.
Love so sweet. Love so unique.
Pure, it guides my feet.
My heart. It controls my beat.
No defeat. Grace and Mercy. It repeats.
Over and over 24 total hours.
Breathtaking, the most beautifulist flower.

I am rhyming, blessing the Most High's love.
Love, love, love, love, love
one 'mo' to begin
question is who's really my friend?
Love so real and 'sho' so why worry?
Interesting being it's not a factor no 'mo'

See, I was once lost and refused to be found.
But for real for real I bless the day that I heard the sound.
Heavenly Father you turned my life around.

Secrets being revealed.
Your love is so personal.
Holy One alone understands how I feel.
Looking out for others as if I have not one need.
Once had a conversation with a bird speaking on how you feed.
Intelligence with a base of vibing kind
Art of existence soothes my mind

God's love. Have not you heard?
Wonderful is the perfect word.
What a mystery that has been repeatedly told
Relax, nowadays ain't nobody worried about being sold.
God's love is priceless.
Bigger than big
Portrayed in rarest forms
even old dusty who takes swigs and dome screams twigs

Father you reached me in order to teach me.

2

All of your perfect ways
Even showed me mad love during haze.
Days of confusion enhanced by satan and his illusions.
Trying oh so hard from the start back in 77.
Creek water baptized age 11


Today, I stand glorifying my man who loves me as Gwen.
He calls me chosen. He calls me friend.
How much do I owe you for what you are placing in my belly?
Father God you favored me even when I was broke, busted, and smelly.


This flow is dedicated to the one and only true God.
Call me loud, peculiar, odd.


Your love is a keeper.
Every day it goes deeper.
I can go on and on.
Lord, you gave me a song
of Faith and it won't be long until this old world gonna be gone.

## I Am Ok

And since I have this invite
let me touch real fast on how you fight.
All my battles result in victory
simply because you love me.

POEM 2

# What Would Jesus Do?

WHAT WOULD JESUS DO if He walked up on you this very hour? Would He be pleased enough to offer you a flower?

Would He smile?

Would He cry?

Would He laugh?

Would He sigh?

What would Jesus do in the middle of your storm?

Would He leave you in the cold?

Would He provide a blanket to warm?

The questions have been raised.
Our Savior is to be praised.
Considering stressful nights, weary days, songs to amaze
Even the filthiest sinner reborn a winner, eating leftover chicken wings for dinner.

What did Jesus do?
What will Jesus do?
How can Jesus and when?
Relax, release, chill out my friend.

Jesus, the prince of peace
My heart, my life, the least
I can give it all to you.
My happiness, joy, when I feel blue.

Do you believe wholeheartedly?
As cleaving to truth?
Remember now, Boaz found Ruth.

So, what would Jesus do?
May I keep it real with you?
Jesus sacrificed just as He was sent.
Calvary, beaten on the cross He went.
So, what did He do?

He stands in the gap for me and you.
He loves and forever on time.
Bet it on up for seasons to shine.

Jesus, I worship You from the depth of my being.
I respect that you ain't deaf and blind cause I
know You be seeing.
All the evil in this world laced with malice,
liars, deceivers living in a worldly palace.

Jesus offers His hand of love, peace, and joy.
Hold on now. Don't get it twisted.
He is not a toy.
He extends the invitation across the nation, the
world, big universe.
All free, girl put away your purse.

Thank you. Thank you for all that you do.
Only because of Your Grace,
My Life is new.

# In the Making

A DAY IN THE MAKING.
Anxiety pressing and shaking.
Trying to understand
the ways of Father God's Hand.
Once feeling lost and alone
words inspiring a song.
From roads of dust and gravel
my future is starting to unravel.
Missing the scene of when y'all needed me.
Now you both believe me.
Praying and speaking words of power
always carried us through hard hours.

A day in the making still proves true.
Just last month, I sat clueless in what to do.

Wherever this found path leads

Father, I will forever remain on my knees.
Wherever you place me firm,
my service I give in return.
Prayers of my parents here.
Restoration because they are near.
Reversing, zig zag, state lines I came.
Dear God, I now know my name.

A day in the making
one who's temp is strange.
Few days back
enemy presented deranged.
Battles no longer have my heart.
If only I knew this from the start.

POEM 4

# I Am Encouraged

FROM THE DIRT ROADS of Mississippi
to the dirt roads of Alabama
On to the concrete jungles of urban Alabama
I came

Even though I have experienced a variety of valleys in my 44 years of existence
I am still here.

God showed me at a very young age that I am a beautiful flower.
I felt that my journey had taken all of the petals and existed only as a stalk.
I never stopped believing.

My dad was forced to leave
Mom speedily married Earlee all at my tender
age of 14.
Searching for stability and family
My journey began

My first time having intercourse at 17.
I became pregnant with my son.
Graduated high school with honors and went on
to college.
Age 21, I became pregnant with my daughter
while living on a college campus.
From there, my journey continued.

Along the way, my petals were still there but I
could not see it.
After two divorces, ex street life, felony convic-
tion, backsliding seasons, drug use, drug sell-
ing, broken heartedness, heart breaking, love
chasing, faith walking, hope keeping, learning
humility.
I am here today.
I am walking forward.
I am letting go of my past.
I am vibrantly seeing all of my petals again

and I am encouraged.

POEM 5

# I Am Redeemed

YOU KNOW, A FEW years ago,
my mess chased me down.
I stumbled.
I fell.
Darkness was my choice to hang around.
I made my bed hard in which I had to lay.
Didn't give a crap about much.
Barely even thought to pray.

You know thinking back during my madness
Now allows me to recognize other's sadness.
Chasing a feel good that is null and void.
Broken, emptiness, a soul deployed.
Just gone off on the deep end.
You ain't fooling nobody.
Your face screams pretend.

All of a sudden, reality sets in.
Reality check. What friend again?

Down rock bottom feeling pitiful?
But God. Forever merciful.

Redemption can too be your jam.
Fill in the blank following I AM.
You are what? No longer a loser.
BUT believe in the words you speak.
Scream, I am strong in the midst of feeling weak.
Change the beat, denounce defeat, refuse to repeat, embrace the heat, taste the cake. God's love is sweet.

POEM 6

# Seen Not Heard

YESTERDAY I WAS BLESSED by
a bird
as my reminder, seen not heard.
Much wisdom from a tree.
It spoke volumes to me.
Your will for my life and being
perfect vision futuristically seeing

The vision already displayed.
The way already made.
Seen and not heard.
Put on display to share your Word.
Allow you to block the evil eye.
Onlookers still asking why.

Father God
thank You for keeping me unseen.

# I Am Ok

Purified now, squeaky clean
so that only Your voice is heard.
Years of pain incurred.
For such a season as this
Holy Spirit filled bliss.

Fill me up God.

# Dad of the Babies

I HEARD HOW DOWN YOU sounded the other day around town.

Remember the days of red noses and big shoes clown.

Some bodies warned you of what would be.

That weed and Hennessy got you in this place currently.

No don't start. Please allow me to complete.

Listening to your sister doesn't make you weak.

I have a heart to say what needs to be said.

Just because of the invite you need to stay out her bed.

It's a trap and it leads to hell.

Don't take my word. Let the Holy Bible tell.

Without your minds, black man we will no longer exist.
Pick up the Word and retract your fists.

Why in the world would you take out your own brother?
Why in the world do you continue to stress out your mother?
You are so right.
We need to let you lead and tell us how to flow.
You the baby daddy, so how we end up po (poor)?

All these students out here looking like they kin.
You think it's funny and blaming it on gin.
What an ugly sin my friend but then I begin to trace this thang all the way back.
My legs were once up in the seat of a black Cadillac
so how can I sit here and finger point?
Let me stay in my lane and walk the way I am anointTED, which led me to write this piece to release a special kind of love. Honestly, it had to come from above.

I am speaking to the baby dad.

Pretty much I have had
it up to here.
Lie on lie in my ear.

Hey man, brother, son, uncle, father, grandpapa,
cousin, and friend.
Wake the F up.
Do we see what state we are in?
I ain't just talking about the SIP.
Listen to the words coming across my lips.
Please, I am pleading for you to stop the bleeding behind all the pain of being insane cause of your last name that you detain and blowing out of brains leaving your baby to be raised by Lil Mane.
Stop the madness because this type of sadness
will have multiple cold bodies lying on tables
and future generations fighting just to be able to
remember your face.

This coming from a sister concerned about her
race.

# Mom of the Babies

YOU KNOW I KNEW I would one
day get this chance.
Perhaps by circumstance
that I been where you are.
Not long ago I couldn't even afford a used car.
The precious life that relies solely on you.
Baby mama this one is for you.

My being is reaching beyond the point of acceptance energy.
See it all stirred back when before synergy.
The struggle and the pain just didn't start with
your name nor the lane in which you reside
Any hood in the USA that joker tends to slide
Hold on now.

Wait before you speak.
Who is to blame for you falling weak
to all his lies and deceit?
You gave him chance after chance when you saw
it was a façade.
Now you're stuck trying to figure out who to
subpoena, James or Rod.

My beautiful dear sister, daughter, mother,
niece, aunt, grandma, and friend.
Why is it so hard to see the state that we are in?
The time has now come for us to dismiss the
drama we come from.
Our little ones are struggling to find their way.
They are ours no matter what the paternity test
say.

Mother of the kids
Cooking chicken, playing wizz, braiding wigs,
taking swigs, living on the edge, hoping for the
best, falling asleep, trying to pass a test.
My love is pouring from a river that is flowing.
It is time to see just what the future will be
if we do not take a stand and do our part for the
betterment of man.

POEM 9

# Poverty Is A Tick

THAT HOOD STORE WITH the faded sign everyday tend to remind me of the customers and patrons who flock
the crap and sugar snacks old dude stock.
It is the heart of the community that depends on once a month income
and it is a true blessing if lil mama make it to prom.

Poverty is a tick and it continues to stick
to our people from years to years
after all the sweat and tears.

Release from the insect is what I speak.

Just because you stumbled seven days last week
It is no reason to stall.
How many times I gotta say it y'all?
You 'gon' be ok.
You hear what I say?
Decision has to be made today.

# False Friend Called Linger

I WOULD FLICK A FINGER toward the one I called linger.
You try to run a play and then one day
it all came to a head.
There was an islander on her sick bed who was
led to send me a warning sign
simply to remind
me of red flags already seen.
You know what I mean?

You are what I called linger and your energy is
a bell ringer
to let the real know to be watchful and wise.
Please have a seat with them fake cries.

I thank you for finally saying what you felt.
I was raised to always smile and wear a belt.

It is all good in the neighborhood.
Roll up with drama. I wish you would
but then I speedily see that anything that affects
my sanity
is just not worth the thoughts and honestly you
ought to just tread light. All love over here. I
been hung up the belt to fight.

Let's continue on with the work that is needed.

POEM 11

# Dumpster Onsite

JUST THE OTHER NIGHT, I heard the big truck back up and beep.
Often why they never consider sleep
for all the ones who hear the sound.
When I threw that sign out, I heard a loud pound.

See the dumpster onsite located to the right of the spaces to park.
Creepy crawlers and stray cats lurk when dark.
Dumpster onsite is a good thing.
Attracting demonic influences has a good ring.

Attract in order to transport for destruction.
Stay tuned. Many blessings in production.

I can't quite see the silence of the dumpster onsite.
From now on let's see wrong as well as right.

Time goes on and produces new crop
but throwing rocks, hiding hands, y'all really need to stop.
I simply will not stoop to allow other's poop to invade my nose.
Peace and love is what me and mine chose.

I am about to settle in my friend before I begin
to really snap and clap with unnecessary flow.
I stood before that criminal judge and agreed to no more.

So shout out to the dumpster onsite.
Let it go. Now take flight.

# Not To Be Erased

ANYONE EVER RECALL PERHAPS a day that stands out to all?

Times in life that now have a reason, perhaps a day week or season.

Anybody else remember perhaps an accident, body dismember.

Early fall, September, or maybe July, brings us to this point call cry.

I strongly agreed, and believed that certain stuff not to be erased that sting from the can call mace is not meant to be erased.

Categories, boxes, seasons, all written in placed.

Any soul reflect back some days perhaps a loving person who encouraged a change of ways.

What's going on? That dry well propels a song.
Hurry, quickly snap back or I won't be long. Egg
frying in the pan, mind gone
And to restate what the vibe hopes to make is a
change and challenge to take
Not to be raised yet instead, truth in faith, so we
all may embrace the freedom is of expression,
and how your pain can be a blessing to someone
of far. Hutu may be struggling being call tar.
Baby is crazy. How we all tend to be lazy, wanted
to be driven like Daisy lol yeah. Poetry amaze
me as well country bumpkin, or southern belle.
Is this an evil spell?
Keep your story and chase that we race. We all
are important is called the human race. Space.

POEM 13

# She Didn't Ask To Be Here

YOU ACT LIKE YOU don't see a repeat of history.

It's a crying shame you can't ever figure out that girl's last name.

I really wish I could reach back and smack you.

Take accountability now for what she's going through.

She didn't ask to be here that old lady said 1999 the year.

Oh wow, you continue to be insane as that woman who gave you your name.

She didn't ask to be here while you walk around steel wearing shorts that say cheer

leader. How dare you even say the type of mother you are. No way.

You act like you don't see how pride put you in a ditch. Just is a runaway bride.

Really really sad that for years later, you truthfully announce who is dad.

She didn't ask to be here so now see the blessing, testimonies, and power filled from past stressing.

You see, although she didn't ask to be here and life been hard. Love is love, and sometimes situations have no regard but once the listen has been taught like dad say since bought

I use my power at this hour to intercede, planning, figuring out fulfilling needs.

Often the cry that is silent, is more loud shoplifting, stealing, lost in crowds.

She didn't ask. Neither did I. So what now? We need an alibi.

No, I want an answer for my kind past time to cancel the dime with satan and all his minions.

 I'm requesting you to listen to my opinion.

Your past is your past. How long will the pity party last?

POEM 14

# Season Of Reason

ACCELERATION TO GREATNESS, FAST forward pace, it's a war cry for the human race. 2023 is purposed to face.

Season of reason in full effect, which now includes the underdog, as well as reject. Grab hold. Let us all reflect.

Smiles, rebirth, stirring up gifts. I witness in the sky; the word shift tune in to the station called uplift. Season of reason has tapped you on the shoulder. Relax, receive the gift of growing older. Let's get busy, shoulders square, stepping bolder.

Energies being released on impressive levels, proclaiming victory, chopping necks of devils.

Season of reason, water has stirred, break-through, deliverance, now you've heard.

# I Am OK

EXCUSE ME.
You gonna be ok.
You think God sent you this way without purpose for today?
I know you don't feel too good.
You think it's helping by puffing that wood.
Excuse me.
You gonna be ok.
You tired and sleepy got a lot on your mind.
Scrapping up that change for that cigar and dime
Excuse me.
You gonna be ok.

You seem like you can't function without popping that pill,
chasing that high.
You done skipped a few meals.

Excuse me.
You gonna be ok.
You hear what I say?
You got that wine beside your bed,
demonic suicide thoughts in your head.
Your neighbor downstairs found dead.
You desperate to escape but scared to thread.
Pondering over kiddie games, Simon said.
Grandma a preacher but fornicating with Deacon Red.

Just stop!
Stop it!
You gonna be ok.
Decision had to be made today.
You been down too long.
It's time for a new play.

Change is calling.
Have you not got tired of falling?
There is a power that is available at any hour
to push you into NEW.
Yeah you.
New ways of thinking.
Gone take a bath and stop stinking.

# I Am Ok

Don't worry about what so and so said.
Wake up. Wake up.
it's time to get out that bed
of self defeat.
Dress yourself up, pull up a seat.
It's time we eat this meat.

See, you gonna be ok.
Because you are hand picked.
See, old lucifer is full of tricks.
Stand in truth and shame his being.
Read the Bible and develop eyes all seeing.
All the scars and wounds from your past
Your joy is here!
This little trouble won't last
long, your testimony is your song

You hear what I say?
Say it with me,
I AM OK

POEM 16

# Keep Living

Excuse me. Listen as I speak.
Emotions rattling tends to makes
muscles weak.
All that crying, spying, lying
mixed with the smoke.
Familiar fries with a stench of artichoke.
Just last week you told Pastor you was woke.
Pass me that iron. It's time to poke.
Have you a clue as to what to do?

No matter how dark the day may seem
Keep living.
No matter how dim the spark may seem
keep living.
Open your heart and learn the art of forgiving.

Do you remember what you said?

It was a flashing yellow light turned red.
All that hurt and revenge is now your past.
Addressing Dr. King, are we free at last?
Removal of mask
what a friend to hath
Secure in our Father's arms, enemy shall do no harm.

Keep Living.

# Family Folk

THIS ONE IS STRAIGHT up, not to
be taken for a joke.
I am the voice for certain family
folk.
Traditions and tales of hand dug wells and dis-
eased cows for sale.
I long to embrace the face or perhaps the place
that influenced adding me to the race.

Family folk from all around town.
A couple of us are caramel, others dark brown.
I once heard something about trees that would
talk.
Auntie and cousin have a similar walk.
Family folk sticking stronger than any glue.
I asked the question, already having a clue.

The strength attached to the last name.
The power of understanding, the importance of
being sane,
Family folk from the same element.
New construction.
Land development.

There is no reason to explain this new season.
If I had to guess, I would surely rest
in the fact of the power from on High.
Dressing in black, fake hugs
when folk die.

I will use my gift, perhaps to shift
the beat of this side.
See, uncle recognized. He saw me in a new ride.
Without compromise, I now smile.
Grab a chair. I'm here for a while.

# So You Can See

THE BEAUTIFUL SUNSET ON any rainy afternoon,
Summer month, let's focus on June.
There is a lily nearby. Please claim it as your flower.
No man will ever know the day or hour.
Being able to see the brink of a new day is truly a blessing.
Say goodbye to former years of stressing.

Sometimes it takes something to happen.
Getting together to discuss the caption should be last on list.
Getting together should never involve fists.
Being drawn by an old song of sadness mixed with defeat.

# I Am Ok

Wake up, 2023 family folk rocking to a new beat, minus the meat from oink.
Bottles of tears on standby to anoint.

Family folks let us all join hands just like a team.
No more name calling because cuz had a bad dream, little sister ripped from zipper to seam, uncle pulling up playing gangsta lean.
Just stop.
Here we go. A new bottle to pop.
Family folks, fighting not to choke the life out of kin.
Gen curse with a stench of gin.

New day. New dawn.
Sleep less. Prevent the yawn.
Time to put in the personal shifts in order to uplift
the ones on their way and unfamiliar with a family day.
The water has stirred, just in case you haven't heard.
Time for us all to do our own part
and in case you haven't noticed... I am writing from my heart.

POEM 19

# Best Of My Entire

THE BENCH IN THE park in Arlington had a special feel.

Little did I know exactly what would be revealed.

I once again found my space of peace.

The best of my entire was beginning to release.

A special event that did take place.

I defeated a veteran in a foot race.

A pure friendship without extra heat,

Best of my entire, I began to shift my feet.

It is a powerful fact that God is able to fulfill any lack.

Best of my entire has a taste that's bold.

Lining up with all the advice from the folks that were old.
Always do your best and God takes care of the rest.

It is time to shine.
The lady was sent to remind.
Ears opened to incline.
Peace. It don't cost a dime.

# I Am Changed

ALTHOUGH IT TOOK A world-
wide shook for me to come into
knowing.
I have a couple of grays in my dome now showing.
I am changed.
Being confined to that small dwelling,
dishes dirty, laundry smelling.

I decided it was time.
I skipped two states.
I am not lying.
I am changed.
Handling legal business via app Zoom,
couldn't afford a mop or broom.

Oh my, if may only tell half,
I was robbed by a Haitian

and I laughed.

He asked why was I alone.

My response sent him on home.

I am changed. Thoughts rearranged. I don't handle people the same.

There is no need to call anyone out of their name.

If you ask me I say that is lame.

Let's all just speak life into each other. Let's get back to when it was easy to trust your brother.

I am changed. I hope you are too. Just in case you may be confused in what to do.

Look up.

# About The Author

A POET FOR SUCH A time, Gwendolyn Michelle Lacy was born in 1977 in Columbus, Mississippi. She grew up in rural Alabama and attended school in both Alabama and Mississippi. Her parents divorced unexpectedly during her early teens, which started her journey of life. Gwen recognized her passion of writing at the precious age of five. She used her gift to create a world of survival, and now at the age of 46 she is sharing it with the world.